Listen to Love

REFLECTIVE POEMS FOR ALL SEASONS

By Alda St. James

LISTEN TO LOVE

Reflective Poems for All Seasons

Alda St. James

Alda St. James

ENDORSEML

"Lov
heal
em
an

"The lyrical poetry Alda writes vividly paints p
thoughts. Her delightful description of her precious d(
feel right there with her. You'll feel her frustration in her
children to listen to the love that is right there ready for th
advantage of. You will feel her passion about the healing
hugs. You can experience the beauty of nature in he
descriptions. This thoughtful, uplifting book will bring you j(
allow you to contemplate life as seen through her eyes."

Emily Thiroux Thr

Author, Loving and Living Your Way Through Gr(

"These poems bring my imagination to those beautiful dry season
days on Lake Malawi."

The Very Reverend Monsignor Andrew Chunda

Malawi, Africa

"Ranging from heartfelt to playful, this poet's debut impressively
explores a range of human experiences in her poems. She displays
keen insight and skill in expressing herself. Readers will find much
enjoyment and opportunities for reflection in this touching
collection of poetry"

John B. Sinclair

President, The Sheridan Foundation

it! So beautiful! Alda St. James' prophetic voice tugs at the and unearths pearls of wisdom found within. Her words race and empower with comfort, hope, and joy. Alda is a gifted artistic storyteller!"

Lori Stanley

Executive Director of Loyola Institute for Spirituality, Orange, CA

The wake-up calls in this extraordinary body of work seem to perfectly balance hopes and dreams with the underlying wisdom of nature and the infinite power of love.

Shirlee Newman

Educational Specialist in California and Hawaii

"The beautiful poetry written by Alda is from the heart and soul…her words will touch each person deeply and uniquely with expressions of grief and comfort. These poems will help you walk through sorrow to healing, even laughter and joy!

Gail Mitchell

Retired Chairman of the Board of Directors, Central Oregon Community College, Bend OR, Head concierge and Les Clefs d'Or member, Sunrise Resort, now owned and managed by Hyatt Hotels

"Thank you for sharing these wonderful poems with me. I like the lovely variety…from a deep poem about love, to a warm and healing poem about hugs, to a playful poem about the author's dog! Delightful! Her poem, From Sorrow to Healing, speaks of her personal journey this year. Beautiful!

Glenda Campos

Spiritual Director, Formation Instructor & Retreat Presenter

"Great book! These poems encourage the reader to contemplate the meaning of life, spirituality, everyday experiences, and death. Readers are led to reflect on these powerful words and draw out their own thoughts, feelings, and experiences".

"The book title and cover images resonate through the moving brilliance of the words within. I have goosebumps! Thank you for sharing these poems. I am truly honored".

"Lovely! Warm and Funny! Rooted in Truth, just like Alda! What a pleasure to recite and ponder."

Copyright

Listen To Love:
Reflective Poems for All Seasons

ISBN: 978-1-7367401-0-1 (kindle)

ISBN: 978-1-7367401-1-8 (Print Book)

First Edition – May 2021

Published by: Prisma Press

Theme illustrations by: Alda St. James

Book design, formatting, publishing & layout by: Exponential Digital Trainers

Email: exponentialdigitaltrainers@gmail.com

DEDICATION

In loving memory of my husband and twin soul,

James F. St. James

OTHER BOOKS BY
ALDA ST. JAMES

---

1. Wisdom Lessons for Today:

   Timeless Words of Inspiration and Instruction

2. Birthstone Coloring Book: *Birthstone Legends and Other Gem Folklore*

   Get A Free Copy: "Birthstone Coloring Book: Birthstone Legends and Other Gem Folklore"

Get Your Free Book Here: https://aldastjames.com/

ACKNOWLEDGMENT

Deep appreciations to:

Anne Gachuhi, without whose patience and understanding this book would not have been possible.

Jeff, Daniel, Nonnie and Carlos, for your unwavering support and enthusiasm. Heartfelt thanks also go to the many dear friends in my life, both near and far, who stepped forward when I needed them most.

TABLE OF CONTENTS

PROLOGUE

T his book has reached completion precisely at the one-year anniversary of my husband Jim's passing. And of course, I still grieve. My new role as published author has brought much comfort though, as I continue to navigate an unfamiliar world called widowhood. The importance of having my children, grandchildren, and close friends in my life, ever ready to support and assist me, cannot be overstated. Without them, this book would not have been possible.

During this past year, I have discovered that there is still much more I want to say. Surely there will be many more poems to write and many new messages to impart. The challenge of this prospect fills me with anticipation, with each new day providing its own unique opportunity for creativity and growth. This is true for all of us. If we are willing to approach life with the attitude of gratitude and expectancy, we invite all the goodness that is in the world to accompany us on our journey.

Life is too short and too precious to waste it, dwelling on things that are unproductive, or worse, downright destructive. It is my hope that

my poems have contributed in some small way to the reader's personal experience of renewal, happiness, and peace. I humbly advise everyone to pay attention to the inner promptings of Spirit, and to always take the time to, *"Listen to Love."*

INTRODUCTION

T he collection of poetry you have before you describes a journey that spans 50 years. As you can imagine, this means I have been writing poetry practically all my life. Yet I never thought about publishing it; rather, my work was a private thing, something I did for fun or therapy, something to share with my husband and closest friends. Little did I know that my first real poem, composed in 1969, was the start of a creative adventure that would manifest spontaneously throughout the ensuing years.

As time passes, "life happens." My husband, Jim, and I met as undergraduate art majors at Syracuse University. Our favorite song in college was "Watching and Waiting" by the Moody Blues, but we also loved dancing the swing, the samba, and the polka. After graduation, we married and moved to California with everything we owned squeezed into an old but serviceable van which Jim had remodeled for cross-country travel.

Arriving as young idealistic artists, we started from scratch what would become a successful custom jewelry business. Over the years, we owned and operated retail stores in California and Colorado. After some time, we decided to relocate to Hawaii. Since Jim was an avid surfer, this move was a no brainer for us. Because of our business success, we wanted to give back to the community in some

way, so at that time, we made the decision to enter the world of foster care.

When we became foster parents, we quickly learned the painful reality of what happens to the unfortunate ones who are caught in the system. Eventually, we adopted three children, a girl and 2 boys. I wrote poetry sporadically during this period, since there was little time for quiet reflection. Make no mistake, there were some very rough years ahead raising these children, and you will see that clearly reflected in the poems I wrote at the time. Luckily for me, I was a professional goldsmith, and I had the freedom to design unique jewelry pieces for my clientele. This kept me balanced and it kept my creative energy flowing.

Despite the difficulties, this family enterprise of creating a "forever family" became our new passion. In 1995, we were selected Hawaii's "Family of the Year." In Honolulu, a gala event was held in our honor. Our family got to ride in a limousine and do a TV interview. We all sang, "We are Family" on stage.

Eventually, Jim and I landed a full-time, shared position to recruit, train, and license foster parents for Maui County. This was a state sponsored program which was meant to equip parents with the tools they needed to become successful foster or adoptive parents.

The experiences we gained doing this work led us to start, in 2005, a non-profit on Maui called Keiki Kokua. In Hawaiian this translates as, "Help the Children." At Keiki Kokua, we owned and operated a Thrift Store which employed foster and former foster youth. We put

on events designed to give foster and adopted children happy memories. Our mission was to do something to mitigate the negative effects of their past, to help heal the painful memories which had lodged in their hearts. This was gratifying work, and we loved doing it.

During this time, when I found time to write, I usually didn't bother showing the poems to anyone. And that was OK, since the act of creative writing, by itself, is its own reward. This is because putting the finishing touches on a poem made me feel whole and complete. I felt like a master chef who has just accomplished a culinary "coup de ta!" Writing poetry has always been like that for me. If sharing happened to happen, I was often surprised and delighted by the response. Apparently, my poems had touched the hearts of those who heard them.

It is worth noting that Jim and I are truly twin souls. We were born on the same day and year, 12 hours apart. And we did everything together. So, you can imagine the shock we felt when in 2017, we learned that Jim had prostate cancer, a most aggressive kind, the same kind that had killed his father. We spent the rest of our time together doing everything we could to arrest the disease, from laser ablation and immunotherapy to radiation and chemotherapy. We adopted a Keto diet, and I began juicing vegetables.

We also prayed continuously for Jim's healing and we asked many others to do the same. We had started a healing ministry at our church which began, coincidently, just before we received the cancer diagnosis, and so we doubled down, continuing to meet

weekly and commit ourselves to prayer with a small, dedicated group. Ultimately, COVID-19 put an end to that.

Gradually, I found myself becoming a full-time caregiver. I embraced this new role with joy; it was a privilege to serve Jim, who was indeed, my other half (he always said I was his better half). Nevertheless, despite everything we did, the disease progressed unabated.

Jim's last week on earth was spent at the Hale at Hospice Maui. Hale is simply the Hawaiian word for house. The care he received there was exceptional. The staff treated us like Ohana, a word often used here to honor caring people who, although not part of your own family, treat you as kindly as if they were. The season of Lent had ended, and it was the beginning of Holy Week when Jim entered Hospice. After 47 years in a loving marriage, he died peacefully in his sleep on Holy Saturday, April 11, 2020. I believe Jim spent Easter Sunday rejoicing in heaven!

At about the same time, COVID-19 had arrived in earnest in Hawaii. Hospice closed its doors to all visitors immediately. This meant that the following Monday, I would not have been able to visit Jim any longer. How blessed we were to be able to be with each other to the end!

Today I am making a new life for myself. It hasn't been easy. After Jim's passing, I suddenly had more free time than ever before, and I pondered what to do with it. Because of the pandemic, volunteering was off limits.

In the beginning, I floundered, doing busy work just to keep myself shielded from the pain. Still, when the invitation came to publish my poetry, it caught me by surprise since, as I already said, my poems had always been a private affair, something I did just for myself, and shared rarely with others. Then something extraordinary happened: after I decided to publish, I immediately began writing again, almost non-stop! It soon became obvious that this was to be my new calling. I am grateful to you, the reader, for accompanying me for a short while on this amazing, creative journey which I now undertake with a tranquil heart.

THEME 1

REFLECTIONS

REFLECTIONS

AWAKE

Why does the melody

That I once sang sweetly,

So sweetly in slumber,

Now reverberate loudly

Through the chambers of my mind?

Yet even as I ponder this

My eyelids are not heavy

For want of sleep...

Because within darkness dwells the fear

Those eyelids shut are plastic stones

Under which Awareness seeks to hide her tears

Still, it was not until
The old man became accustomed to drowsing
By the ticking of the clock
That I realized, I too,
Would lie here awake,
Listening to this strange music
As it gradually fades
Into twilight sleep...

WANTING MORE

Nothing is new to me
Each day is the same
What I am told
I've heard before
Where I go
I've been before
The things I want
I've wanted and had
And having had
I've wanted more

Everything's new to me
Each day filled with delight
Each word a key
To some new thought
Each place unique
For its special charm
The more I see
The more I want
And having had
I still want more

TO JIM

When I look at you
Really look
Past your image
There is something greater
Something more
It speaks to my soul
Speaks softly
To my soul

You are not showy
But humble
Sometimes to the extreme
You refuse to compete
For the attention of men
In this aggressive world
I think we both know
You would lose anyway

It is just this fact
That in an instant
Opened my eyes
To see who you really are
The very essence of love
The fullness of life
The richness of creation
The goodness of humanity

PARADOX

Attachment is a good thing
Yet we must become detached
From all things that hinder

Self-esteem is a good thing
Yet we must esteem ourselves less
So we can become more

A strange paradox indeed
That what we strive for
Thinking healthy and right

Becomes at a certain point
Something to lose
In order to gain

AT THE ABBEY

Finally....
The aimless routine of daily life
Gives way to the gentle rhythm
Of this peaceful, sacred space

Truly...
I hear God's voice in the flowing river
He speaks of many things
But not in words

Here...
Where time is not, yet there is never enough
I soak in the essence of this place
In communion with all that is

MY SHADOW

Running after my shadow
Away from the sun
I move, it moves,
But always at a distance
I never catch up to it

My shadow
Wants to go one step ahead
Just one step in front of me
To touch the darkness
I must wait until sunset

<u>GOD IS LOVE</u>

Your Movement is Stillness
Your Way, Solitude
Your Voice is Soundless
Your Language, Silence
Your Threshold is Watchfulness
Your Pathway, the Will

For without Will
There is no Desire
Without Desire
There is no Passion
Without Passion
There is no Intimacy
Without Intimacy
There is no Love
Without Love
There is no God

It is because of Love
That God exists
And because of God
Love exists
God is simply
Another name for Love

THEME 2
A PURE HEART

A PURE HEART

YOUR LIGHT
When I am with you
There is a light
Which has no name
Is it wisdom?
Is it grace?
Or are they
Both the same?

When I see you
I see something
That sets apart
You from others
What can it be?
A kind soul?
A gentle heart?

When I touch you
There is a glow
That shines so bright
What is this thing
So soft and pure?
It is my beacon
Through darkest night.

LISTEN TO LOVE

Listen to Love, my children
He calls to you!
Listen to Love, my children
He speaks to you!

Why won't you open your ears?
Why won't you open your hearts?

Listen to Love, my children
He wants you!
Listen to Love, my children
He begs you!

But you won't hear him, will you?
And you don't feel him, do you?

How then, can you trust?
How then, can you believe?
How then, can you ever
Listen to Love?

ESTRANGED

It is so tempting to cling to
Things that hurt so much
Is our pain so precious?
That we will not let it go?

Oh, may I have strength to
Endure that awful pain
Then banish it from memory
And I will think of it no more!

Only then can I emerge
Purified in mind and heart
Freed from the bondage
That no longer entraps me.

IF I HAD A PURE HEART

If I had a pure heart

There would be no ego to defend

No hope for retaliation

No resentment to harbor

No agenda to pursue

If I had a pure heart

IF I LOVED YOU

If I loved You
As You love me

You would open my eyes
That I might see
Beyond the veil
Life's mystery

You would open my ears
That I might hear
The silent music
Of the spheres

You would open my mind
That I might find
The splendor
That is so sublime

If I loved You
As You love me

WHO IS GUILTY?

When You say,

"Father forgive them,

For they know not what they do."

Who then, is deemed guilty?

Or who then, is innocent?

If I say to my enemy,

"I forgive you."

He may feel free to hurt me again.

So, was his guilt removed?

Or has it just been reinstated?

Who is Guilty?
Footnote: Based on Luke 23: 34

FORBEARANCE

Just as there is some good
In every person,
There is some benefit
In every path taken.

Humanity Is evolving
As it moves relentlessly
Toward the purpose
For which it was created.

Do not judge another
Or criticize that which
Is foreign to you, and
You don't understand.

Your path may be
Better, higher, nobler,
Yet their path too,
Contains some hidden merit.

So bear with those
You would condemn,
Give each one
The room to grow.

That is precisely
What your heavenly Father does,
Then how unexpected and delightful
When their wayward path leads to good!

Unless of course,
By obstinate power of will,
Their path, instead
Leads to Hell.

In which case, do forewarn
But do not insist,
For a man can and must choose
His preferred destiny!

THEME 3
LOVE

LOVE

THE PUZZLE

As we sleep
We fit together perfectly
Like the complex puzzle
Which is our lives

As we sleep
We blend in a way
That forms a splendid portrait
Of love personified

As we sleep
The disparate pieces of ourselves
Merge together to rest
In heavenly repose

A CONTEMPLATION OF EASTER

The law of love, so unrelenting
It's quest – so absolute
The foes of love, so unrepenting
The voice of love stands mute!

The gift of love, so oft' rejected
The gift for which He died
The gift of love, He so perfected
Yet by most, denied.

In sorrow, the light of love grows dimmer
In patience it gains reward
And though the glow be just a glimmer
There's hope in love restored!

Be joyous then, on Easter day
Though love be bruised and torn
In Him who lives and lights the way
In Him is love reborn!

So surely will our love endure
Hardship and dejection
And just as surely, He assures
Our final resurrection!

You are kind in all your actions
Tender in your ways
I love you more than ever
I offer you my praise.

For giving me your precious love
When I have felt alone
You are gentle, like a dove
The greatest joy I've known!

LOVE POEM 1

When the day is done
The setting sun
Reminds me of you

The stars above
Their cosmic love
Turns me back to you

Near despair
A hope and prayer
Tell me to trust in you

The ocean roar
The distant shore
Bring me home to you

The birds that sing
Each new spring
Shows me that I love you more

LOVE POEM 2

My love is real
My love is true
My love is here
Just for you!

My heart is large
My spirit bowed
My body charged
LOL!

You are the one
You know you are
You are my sun
My shining star!

A LOVE WALTZ

Well, I know it's true
What I see in you
A love that's sweet and kind
I can see
It was meant to be
A love so sublime
A love that's truly mine

The love we share
Is beyond compare
It is God's own design
I know it's true
When I look at you
A love almost divine
A love transcending time

In all we do
Our love is true
A fault you cannot find
From whence we came
We are just the same
Our stars they do align
A very special sign

Well, it's plain to me
That we must be
A love so pure and fine
I clearly see
It's destiny
A love beyond all time
A love for all mankind

SPRINGTIME!

Love is in the air!
Love is everywhere!
In the blossom
In the trees
In the gentle, springtime breeze!

Love is in your eyes!
Love tells me no lies!
In your words
In your smile
In your own, distinctive style!

Love is in that fruit!
Even though it's mute!
In the peach
In the cherry
In the apple, fig, and berry!

Love is truly here!
We shall have no fear!
Despite our struggles
In our strength
Abides a steadfast, quiet faith!

Let's hail this splendid morn!
Let us be reborn!
In this time
In this place
May we claim abundant grace!

ON VALENTINE'S DAY

I love you truly
You must understand
I love you more
Than anyone can

I love you so much
More than I show
I love you dear
And I want you to know

You are my heart
My prayer each day
You are my joy
Beside you I'll stay

Forever and more
Forever you'll be
Friend and lover
My eternity

THEME 4
COSMIC AWARENESS

COSMIC AWARENESS

HIDING ONE'S LIGHT

Black and gray veils
In a barren land
Keep a wellspring
Of joy deep inside

Hiding one's light
When the weather is bad
Is good for the soul
But not for the mind

Oh new moon night!
When secrets are made
Let me learn thy lessons
Without remorse

Hiding one's light
When the weather is good
Is bad for the mind
But not for the soul

<u>UNTITLED</u>
I hear...
The Music of the Spheres

I see...
Beyond the earthly Veil

I feel...
The Love that surrounds me

I am...
A precious child of God

COSMIC SYMPHONY

Have you ever been asked
If you were a musical instrument
What kind would it be?
A blaring trumpet
A winsome piccolo
Perhaps an organ or piano?

To create an orchestra
Many diverse sounds must come together
Many discordant voices must merge
For one purpose only
To produce a harmonious blending
Of tones and texture

Each individual must decide
What position he will play
In the great unfolding Symphony
Each mastering the same universal melody
Each agreeing to play in unison with the others
Coming in and out at precisely the right moments

All must consent to follow
Cues emanating from Primo Maestro
For he is the Master Conductor
He directs the Music of all Creation
The grand Symphony of the Cosmos
Can you hear it?

AWAKENING

It's not that I am moving closer to God
Or Him to me...
It's rather that
I've become aware of Him
In the midst of things...
Color, form, light,
Screaming to be heard...
In the very substance of all
The quiescent fabric of being....
For there is no becoming or arrival
Only Awakening to what already is

THE MASTER ARTIST

Art for art's sake
Is a saying we use
To describe the essential nature of art
The drive to produce a masterpiece
The need to create something beautiful
Solely for its own sake

So too, creation exists for creation's sake
In which the cosmic Artist
Calls forth His exquisite work
As expression of His divine nature
Forever evoking imaginative artistries into being
Inconceivably varied in form and design

These made for the enjoyment of creatures
Of both angels and mortals
Yet it's not adulation He seeks
But simple acknowledgement
Of His dynamic handiwork
Which reflects His very Being

Likewise, as with all true artists
He delights most in sharing
His sublime creativity
Its staggering immensity
Its unfathomable beauty
With all who view it

Yet, art for art's sake
Means no one need witness it
Since both art and creation endure
Despite our awareness of it
Certainly, the artist MUST create
Regardless of who observes

If stupidly, we fail to honor Him
It is indeed our loss
Since recompense
Accompanies praise
Neither will the Creator be recognized
For the Genius that He is

In the end, it is the artists among us
Even perhaps the scientist
Who, in a reflective moment
Authentically marvels at the complexity
The astounding imagination and skill
Of the Master Artist at work

AT THE MONASTERY 1

My body shouts
INTELLIGENCE!
All creatures scream
ALIVE!
Flower, bird, or blueberry
Dog, cat, or crustacean
Proclaim God's awesome Name!
His perfect designs call out
Whispering loudly
Come, come...
Look at us
REALLY LOOK!

The rarest of rarities
Is the Universe
And everything in it
Oh, unholy man!
You have eyes to look
You have mind to know
But you still do not grasp
The magnificence of it all
And the transcendent Reality
Behind the natural world
Remains forever
Beyond your reach

THE SCAFFOLDING

I am the Scaffolding which supports
An ancient, fragile structure
Called Virtue and Righteousness
Daily is this noble edifice rebuilt
Through blood, sweat, and tears
In the lives of people
Who cherish its worth

I am the backbone
Of a spineless generation
Whose companion is greed
And whose byword is fear
I exist only to sustain it
Helping it develop
Into a tougher, truer Self

I am the Confessor
Who listens to souls
Poor, suffering souls
Pleading for mercy
I exorcise their demons
I absolve their past
I bind up their wounds

I am the Buttress
Bearing the full weight
Of hatred and oppression
I lift myself high
Bracing the beams
Providing the cosmic muscle
Upon which all humanity rests

THEME 5
THE NATURAL WORLD

THE NATURAL WORLD

HYACINTH

Flower of the heart

Flower of the mind

The Hyacinth grows

But no one knows

Why she sighs

And why she cries

When winter comes

When all is one

For that is the time

We must wait

For a soothing rhyme

And a turn of fate

If the Hyacinth sighs
And the Hyacinth cries
She must not know
That only in spring
Can she grow
That nothing thrives
At winter's eve
When flower nor leaf
Is left to grieve
For summer is gone
And nature sings
A mournful song

Still the Hyacinth
Will be the last
To loosen her hold
To let go her grasp
If she could stay
During winter's mirth
She knows quite well
She'd be the first
To show her face

Again in spring
Wearing the smile
That sunbeams bring

Impatient flower!
She has to know
Why can't she prosper?
Why can't she grow?
Each of the days
Of every year
Free from worry
Free from fear
Strange bright flower
Not all can see
The Hyacinth is life
The Hyacinth is me

THE CYCLES OF LIFE

A child is like the rising sun,
Song unsung
Which creeps across a cloudless sky,
Somewhat shy
But grows more daring every hour,
Gaining power
As the clock ticks fast away,
Each finds his way,
Finds his way.

Middle age is the craving earth,
Constant thirst
Which walks upon a barren land,
Grain of sand
And does exist just to survive,
Unsatisfied
Yet dwindles all its time away,
And does delay,
Does delay.

Old age is like the waning moon,
Setting soon
Which drifts upon a darken sky,
Death is nigh
And weakens as the end draws near,
Fighting fear
Until at last it fades away,
Then come what may,
Come what may.

The soul is but a shining star,
Seen afar
Which plays upon an endless night,
Seeking light
And finds a place in deepest space,
To contemplate
Before to earth it does descend,
To try again,
To try again.

IT'S SPRING

Birds calling sweetly
Happily courting, mating,
Nestled in the trees

Rain drips on green leaves
Flowers burst into bloom
Everywhere is color

It's Spring!
Footnote: written in "Haiku" style

ODE TO FINDHORN

Full moon night

The garden

A satin finish

Of rocks and thorny bushes

Red ripe berries

Whose time has come

Behold the myriad creatures
Dancing through time!
Elves and fairies
Nymphs and sprites
Ignorant of me
And of themselves

They chant aloud
I know I see
I can I am!
Exploding ears
Shattering mind
Touching soul

REQUIEM FOR THE TREES

I drove by the church today
And saw them
Their heads were chopped off
They died a martyr's death
For the cause of Nature
I cried for them

They gave their lives
For concrete sidewalks
And city ordinances
Now their dead bodies
Once so splendidly dressed
Stand naked in the midst of spring

ARE YOU THERE?

Are You there?
Just beyond seeing
In quiet night
Moonlight beaming
Shooting star

Are You there?
Just beyond knowing
In endless profusion
Of fragrant flower
Luscious grass

Are You there?
Just beyond believing
Bursting forth
From tiny seed
Or joyous song

AUTUMN DAY SPLENDOR

Autumn day splendor
Shimmering sky
Crystal clear brook
Babbling by
Lay back and listen
Let out a sigh
Dare not to ask
Just when or just why
How does one trust
A silent reply?
Keep dreaming of Spring
And let the old die

THE CLOUDS

The clouds roll by
Looming large on the horizon
Moving fast as if positioned
On a heavenly conveyor belt

I watch transfixed
As they travel northward
On an exacting path
Parallel to earth

Their bottoms, a flat, blue line
Their tops, a billowing array of white
Subtly changing shape
Yet somehow remaining unchanged

They glide along effortlessly
A beauteous treat for the eyes
Yet they completely ignore me
As if no one is watching

THEME 6
FAMILY AND CHILDREN

FAMILY AND CHILDREN

OUR FAMILY STORY

This is a time to look back
A golden time to cherish
A season in life to savor
A small place in Eternity

Remember our love beginning?
So simple yet so clear
We two were twins at birth
Joined by Destiny

I knew you so well then
Your energy was boundless
Your kindness won my trust
Your spirit stirred my heart

Married in the sunlight
We were a special pair
Wanting nothing but love
Having nothing, yet satisfied

One day without us knowing
A cloud's dark shadow cast
A tragedy! I could never be
The mother of your child

Sadness overwhelmed me
Until our daughter came
Then unknown voices promised
"Your life is now complete."

We were a little family
For just a little while
Until Awareness grabbed her
And love was not enough

You were patient then, and wise
I was broken-hearted

"How can I go on?" I cried
You said we would – together

Twenty years of living
Two lives appear as one
I remember it like yesterday
When I gave myself to you

Now is a time to look forward
Now is a time to rejoice
To speak those vows again
To love as never before

This is my humble gift
A heart that is resilient
A devotion that is pure
A fidelity that lasts forever

Spirit of Love sustain us
Let us play and laugh once more
Help us dream new dreams for the future
Bring us closer to each other and You

<u>NONNIE</u>

My beautiful child of three
Brings out the child in me
Watch how she plays
Her carefree ways
My beautiful child of three

My lovely daughter of three
Brings out the love in me
A warm embrace
Her shining face
My lovely daughter of three

My sweet little girl, Nonnie
Will always bring joy to me
A budding rose
Heaven knows!
My sweet little girl, Nonnie

MY CHILD

A simple thought
On Valentine's Day
To let you know
That because of the joy
And despite the pain
I am still your mother
After all

You may never write
Forget to call
I may not know
Where you are
It hurts a lot
Just waiting for
Someone you love to care

Once more, I quiet my heart
Once more, brush away the tears
And I resolve to live my life
As though you weren't there
But as long as it takes
I will watch and wait
For my child to come back home

CHILDREN YOU MUST KNOW

Children you must know
It is not in your Father's nature
To compete with evil
For the attention of his offspring
And it is not in my nature either

TO MY ADOPTED CHILDREN

I do know
What you went through
I was there
Standing by you
Not next to you
But always beside you
Trying and failing
Failing and trying
To help

Still, you resented
Setting the bad times
To memory
And forsaking the rest
I did the opposite
Choosing to remember
The gift of life
I nurtured
When no one else would

Love and forgiveness
Can only thrive
When pride is rejected
Replaced by humility
When self-righteousness
Yields to compassion
For only the humble heart
Can experience hope
Only the humble heart

ON FATHER'S DAY

You are the kind of parent
I always wanted, but never had

I admire the way you love your children
Think hard about what to say and how to help them

It grieves you to leave them alone
When they are cold and distant

And you do it with a grace and kindness
They will never know

But I know...
And I celebrate the Dad that you are

NO CHILDHOOD

When people talk about their childhood
And what they enjoyed most
It makes me think back to mine
How come I cannot recall
My favorite meal, music, or memory?

What I can remember
All too vividly
Is the loneliness
The times of being teased
Times of humiliation

Now, just now, do I realize
I grew up fast and furiously
Without warmth or tenderness
And when I arrived at adulthood
It was a welcome reprieve

But only now, as I look back
Do I truly see how hard life was
Fending for myself as a child
And I am amazed to discover
I really had no childhood at all

THEME 7
SELFISHNESS

SELFISHNESS

THE FIGHT

You led me into a trap
And I fell
Like a wounded animal
You baited me
With your words
I let down my guard
For a lousy second
Just for a second

Then recoiled
From your attack
Impulsively, instinctively
But too late
To avert a confrontation
So fierce, so violent
Which somehow
I had caused

CAREFREE LIFE

Carefree life
Cool and nice
Only I am worth the price

Bones on fire

Turned to ice
So very nice
To hold the dice

And I play to win

Yes, to win
Dice in spin
What is sin

But a work of art?

For boyish grin
Or face of tin
Smooth and trim

Can be my guise

Senses numb
To songs unsung
And deeds undone

What do I care?

Of things begun
Life's my gun
The holy one

And I shoot to kill

Beware you say
There comes a day
When one must pay

For evil deeds

Guilt leads the way
Is that what you say?
Is this God's way?

Just fantasy in your mind

Only fools are caught
With minds distraught
In webs so taut

From anger and hate

If pleasures sought
All things are naught
You must be taught

That you alone matter

Dice be tossed
Innocence lost
Never the cost

Too high to pay

Compassion lost
Whatever the cost
The loser is tossed

Away with the wind

Endless play
It's nature's way
Sweet young prey

Are easy to find

You need only say
I love you today
Come what may

Tomorrow after all, we could die

<u>DEFIANCE</u>
I will not defend myself
Say of me what you will
I keep my love
Tucked deep inside
Quiet as a dove.

Red hot tempers
Ice cold stares
Break my heart in two
You are right, and I am wrong
No way – it wasn't you!

Trampled feelings
Hurtful words
Disrespect and disregard
No apology or concern at all
For making life so hard!

THE CELEBRATION

My son scored a victory today
Against conscience
He is celebrating by erecting
A flag in his room
He has discovered that no one
Can force goodness upon him
Let the celebration begin!

HEART OF STONE 1

How do you move a heart
That's rock hard and stone cold
No kindness,
No mercy?

How do you change a mind
That's rigid, unyielding
Close-minded,
Vengeful?

How do you free a soul
That's caught in a trap
Of hatred,
And self-loathing?

Ultimately it is with love
A loving indifference
Requiring nothing of you,
Except not to expect results.

HEART OF STONE 2

Oh heart of stone
Go make your home
In someone else's place
Do not come here
Do not come near
To pierce my sacred space

Oh, heart of stone
You do condone
Every selfish action
You woo your prey
Make him repay
For your satisfaction

You are so vain
It is a shame
You will not do what's right
It seems to me
You cannot see
A glimmer of the light

I know you well
And time will tell
Of what you undertake
Will you atone
Oh, heart of stone
For someone else's sake?

I doubt your word
It is absurd
To trust in what you say
Oh, heart of stone
Leave me alone
And go your separate way

THEME 8
SUFFERING

SUFFERING

OFFENDED

I see you are offended

But did he mean to hurt you?

Or was it just ignorance?

I'm in no position to judge

But I do understand

It always looks different

From the outside

THE CRUCIBLE

Like the refiner's metal
I prepare to enter
The crucible of mortality
To become something more
Or to become something else
I feel the purging flame
The unrelenting heat
The lumps that were my body
Slowly melt and coalesce
Fire engulfs me
And I begin to glow
Like a bright orange ball

When at last
The crucible is emptied
Releasing its precious cargo
I am poured out
At once
Like a libation
And gradually
I cool
Having been changed
Transformed
Into an ingot
Of pure gold

The Crucible
Footnote: based on Sirach 2: 1, 5

WAR

There is no war here
Isn't that incredible?
Just a white cat
With pink ears
That cries at night

FAMINE

There is no famine here
We have all we want
But there is this white cat
With pink ears
That cries at night

<u>WEEPING</u>

Alone in pain and sorrow
Like Bernadette
John of the Cross
Like Jesus and Mary
I feel your anguish
As you feel mine

I weep
Seeing your eyes
Crying my tears
Weeping for my children
For your children
For us all

IF HUGS COULD HEAL

If hugs could heal
I would squeeze you tight
And not let go
I would hold on forever
Or until you said
Enough...
I am well

If hugs could heal
I would gently enfold you
In a warm embrace
I would keep on saying
I love you, I love you,
And you would say...
I am cured

If hugs could heal
I would be the best hugger
In the whole wide world
I would never stop
Never grow weary
Until all who suffer cry out...
I am free!

REJECTED

They can't understand why You came
Disguised, sharing the poor man's lot
What were You thinking?
People would believe You?
Or did you know they would not?

So why would You, Son of God
Choose poverty when You came?
You know too well
Our human nature
Swoons over wealth and fame.

The one who decides for obscurity
Has removed his sordid mask
And has searched longingly
For You, hidden
In the trash.

Then I knew, you want none of wealth
And fame is its own reward
He who seeks
It is he who finds You
It is he who calls You Lord!

HOMELESS

I want to go home but
I still don't know where I live
Every house is the wrong address
I can't find my way back home

THEME 9
SEPARATION AND LOSS

SEPARATION AND LOSS

CONTEMPLATING SUICIDE

From the moment you were born
You were sentenced to hard labor
None can refute
That you suffer grievously
And certainly no one has it harder than you

Work, rest, eat, sleep,
Repeat, repeat...
So boring, so dull
What reason for this?
Is there no reprieve?

Your heart cries out
But no one answers

And quiet rage –
Your ally in pain –
Settles deep in your soul

The days seem endless
Unbearable, pointless
Without love you languish
Feeling neither joy nor grief
Nor hope nor fear

Pride blocks the change
That would heal your heart
Without love, you implode
I want to know –
How can you live?

TALK TO ME
Talk to me
While you still can
In the midst of illness
In the final struggle

Share the things that matter most
And the things that don't
Tell me about your living
And about your dying

Tell me your story
With all is poignancy
With its dreams and fears
Its loves and losses

I need to know your thoughts
To feel your feelings
To find out who you really are
Before you can no longer speak

<u>BY MYSELF</u>

Eating dinner alone
Table set for one
No one to say
It's tasty or bland
No one to offer
Quiet conversation

No one to share
The daily routine
Oh how I miss you!
How I long for those days!
Which were so easy to come by
But so hard to replace

WHEN YOU DIED

I must admit
Your death was a surprise
Even though you were sick
For two and a half years...
I never really thought you would die
But it was not denial
I just truly believed you would be healed

And we would go on living
As we did before

Yet I also knew, or rather felt
A force within me crying out
"Remember, God is sovereign!"
And deep in my soul I knew....
That despite my pleadings
Despite my wants and needs
He would take you away

In the end I had to accept
That God alone decides

My pain, anguish, grief
Knew no bounds
They followed me everywhere
They were more than I could bear...
But still they were mine
To own and negotiate
To manage and suffer through

In this new reality of being
Of being alone

Immersed in a crushing existence
I clung to a thin hope
As a drowning man
Clings to a rock...
Though I wept bitter tears
Sweet consolations
Came as Signs from Eternity

Signs I could not mistake
For anything other than what they were

I used these Signs
These messages from above
As rungs of a ladder
To lift myself up...
To pull myself out of despair
To discern a new plan for my life
To find meaning beyond my grief

To discover it waiting
Somewhere in the rubble

NO WORDS

How I miss you sweetheart
There are no words to say it
Although I attempt it
No words can convey it!

How I miss your presence
I dwell in darkest night
Adrift in constant longing
What harsh, unhappy plight!

How I miss your laughter
Its absence is my grief
I live my life in mourning
I am indeed bereave!

Not seeing you again
In this earthly orb
Assails my aching heart
Such pain must absorb!

THE VISITOR

I am an inmate of the world
A prisoner of matter
Looking through the small cubicle of my mind
At the Visitor who confronts me

He tells me He can set me free
That I am not condemned to die
Yet I am guilty of all charges
I can offer no defense

His words are somehow muffled
The meaning is unclear
Noisy conversations in the cubicle next to mine
Keep distracting me, I wish I could see His Face!

Suddenly He rises to leave
I regain my concentration
But it is too late, for He is gone
I sit alone wondering why I am here

AT THE AIRPORT

Browsing the newsstands
Wandering the corridors

I am waiting
Just waiting
Just waiting
To get on that plane!

Eating for diversion
Drinking something sweet

As I wait
And I wait
Yes I wait
To board that plane!

There is a line of people
Many ahead of me

While I'm waiting
Still waiting
Just waiting
To get on that plane!

How long must I stand here?
I am keen to depart!

But I keep waiting
Yes waiting
I keep waiting
To board that plane!

I need patience to endure it
And perseverance too

Because I wait
And I wait
I can't wait
To go back home!

THEME 10
PRAYER

PRAYER

ILLUSION

God, I want to touch You!
Why illusion above and below, more illusion?

Is there a reality to grasp?
I cannot live in a world that does not exist!

The dispersion of my bones
Will lead to the solution of this riddle.

If Man is exactly in the middle of nowhere
Then where is this Woman?

Everything sounds like music
Or music sounds like everything.

HOLY HOUR

He speaks...
"Lend me your ear"
"Tune in the radio"
"Can you hear?"

I say yes...
But the message is unclear
Yet I want to embrace it
Right now, and right here!

I remain quiet...
That He might reveal more
Until at long last
He bursts open the door!

Then shimmering light...
Luminous, etheric rays
Proclaim the end of life
Begins Heaven's timeless days!

All sweetness...
Oh, beguiling rays
Shine upon me longer
Your pure, alluring gaze!

Such overwhelming vision ...
Can it really be so?
Indeed, prayer is the key
This much I know.

DO YOU?

Do you see me?
For I am but a grain of sand
On the endless coast of time and space

Do you hear me?
For I am but a quiet voice
Amid the clamor of modern men

Do you know me?
For I am but a tiny mark
Carved upon the palm of your hand

Do you love me?
For I am lost without your care
In the vast wasteland of planet earth

ADAM

I heard You calling
In the Garden
And I hid myself
From Your sight
But that was long ago

Now I search for You
In deepest sorrow
And You hide Yourself
As I once did
So long ago

HELP ME, LORD

Help me Lord
As I kneel and pray
Give me strength
Just for today
Help me walk

Along Your way
Teach me to
Respond and say,
Yes, Lord, yes,
I will obey!

COMPELLED

Compelled by an inner fire
I made the hard right
Almost without thinking

As if a hidden force
Were driving me
To that place of utter stillness

Sense less...
Without thought or sound
Devoid of motion

For an eternal moment
Leaving space and time
Travelling at the speed of light

Only later...
Did I reluctantly return to a world
Consumed by its own importance

<u>JESUS, *please*...</u>
Give me a drop
Of Your patience
As you gave me
A drop of Your suffering
For I am caught
In the dark night
Where no solace is found
Wracked with pain
Crippled in fear
Lost and alone
Amid an alien world
Immersed in self-love

Come then, come quickly!

Soothe my brokenness

Heal my aching heart

Shore up my weak limbs

Give me strength

For I have none

Give me hope

That I may endure

Give me light

That I may see

In the midst of death
Give me Life!

Jesus, please...
Footnote: based on John 19: 16

AT THE MONASTERY 2

You are Lord
Of time and space
You reside
In every place
You are Love
And You desire
To free us all
Caught in the mire

You are King
Of heaven and earth
You decide
Our death and birth
You decree
We suffer and die
A mystery –
But You know why

We trust in You
Hope trumps all doubt
We would be fools
To live without
Abundant faith
A big mistake
Our souls, Oh Lord
Do not forsake

Guide our path
Along the way
Lead us all
Who hope and pray
Sovereign God
We plead our case
Fill us with
Redeeming grace

THEME 11
FINDING TRUTH

FINDING TRUTH

WHERE YOUR TREASURE IS

There is only one Truth
One Treasure
One Pearl of great price
But there are
A million paths to find it

Most roads we follow
Lead nowhere
While others, though promising
Are nothing more
Then dead-end streets

How then, to find your way?
It is as simple as this:
"Where your Treasure is,
There also is your Heart"
In this is great wisdom

For your Treasure IS your Heart's desire
And whatever your Heart desires most
That is where you begin
It will take you to the path
You must follow

But the Heart's most pure desire
Is also the most direct and perfect Way
By moving into that reality
You become your authentic Self
Henceforth this true Self

Leads the way
And merges with the one great Truth
Bestowing meaning and purpose
Revealing at last, the ultimate Treasure
For which we all seek

Where Your Treasure Is
Footnote: based on Matthew 6: 19-21

HEAVEN!

When I go
When I breathe my last
May it not be slow
But brief and fast

When I'm laid low
When my lot is cast
This I know
My Love will last

When at that Gate
With all my heart
I celebrate
N're to depart

What stores await
Celestial art!
Which I embrace
With grateful heart

To know all things
No sin concealed
The bells, they ring
The Truth revealed

The angels sing
Of Truth unsealed
The King of kings
Is Love revealed!

THE CHRIST

He hangs on the Cross
Between good and evil
Between obedience and defiance
Between power and weakness
Between divinity and humanity
Between salvation and despair

He is the Intersection
Of spirit and logic
Of faith and science
Observer and observed
Arbitrating between them
Resolving all things unto Himself

Standing outside of time
He is Alpha and Omega
Beginning and end
The ultimate Solution
The Reconciler
Of all dichotomies

FROM SORROW TO HEALING

Although you live in sorrow
In loss and loneliness
There is a new tomorrow
A chance for happiness

Don't speak of love denied
Allow for openness

Such method will provide
A needed, soothing rest

This leads to tranquil life
It helps assuage the pain
It mitigates the strife
It makes the loss, a gain

Then verily, your light will shine
Your radiance will consume
All fears of every kind
Of misery and gloom

And despite your many trials
From anxiety reframe
When the evil one beguiles
The truth you must retain

This truth must be coaxed
In order to sustain
The truth that love alone invokes
Is more powerful than pain

TO MY FELLOW CHRISTIANS

I don't know why
You would believe a lie
The facts are there to see,
When you break God's law
One or all
You invite iniquity.

If you boast and brag
Belittle and nag
You cannot represent the Lord,
Yes abortion is wrong
But equally so
Are slander, corruption, and fraud.

I cannot ignore
I must deplore
Self-aggrandizement and malice,
Disparage a hero
Insult the weak
How can one be so callous?

So, don't be fooled
By a despot's rule
Of law and order and might,
Discrimination must end
And love alone
Will make our country right.

To this very day
Some will say
Sinners are redeemed by Christ,
You fail to see
That one must be
Humble, meek, and contrite.

So, what you deny
Demands a reply
Says the Lord God of Hosts,
Integrity of mind
A compassionate heart
Are still what matter most

To My Fellow Christians
Footnote: based on James 2: 10, and 2 Timothy 4: 4

IDOL WORSHIP

Who or what
Do you idolize?
Who or what
Do you live for?
Who or what
Can you not live without?

For some, it's a sport legend
A film or rock superstar
Glamour or prestige
Riches and material success
Maybe it's just a mesmerizing video game
Maybe it's Harry Potter

Or it could be...
An irresistible food or drink
A rare delicacy or dessert
It could, of course, be alcohol
It could be sex or drugs
Or all of the above

When this Idol of yours
Becomes your master
As it surely will
You become its willing slave
You are more than happy
To do its bidding

In due time...
The thing your Idol demands
Whether pleasing or disturbing
Becomes harder to resist
You sense a strange power
Forcing you to comply

Remember this...
Whatever your Idol
Happens to be
It rages against you
And without restraint
You are locked in its iron grip

The thing you constantly crave
The thing you'd give anything for
The thing you must possess
Is ultimately the very thing
Keeping a stranglehold
On every aspect of your life

THEME 12
ETERNITY

ETERNITY

WHERE IS MY BELOVED?

Are you seated
At the Banquet table?
Have you tasted
The Heavenly wine?
Have you eaten
The Divine bread?
Pray, tell me...
I long to know!

Where Is My Beloved?
Footnote: based on Luke 14: 15

A TALK TO MYSELF

You know,
You are not perfect,
Not even close,
But you give completely,
You try your best.

When I hear good poetry,
It is like a song,
The message,
Raw and unfiltered,
Still lingers on.

The meaning of eternity,
Is perpetual growth,
When comes that day,
All attributes of virtue,
Are realized in the soul.

THE OBSERVATORY
It's a crystal clear morning
Look up!
Haleakala rises
High in the sky
And without clouds to obscure
The Observatory verily glistens
In brilliant sun

For a moment
It looks like Heaven
I wonder,
Is God observing me?
For I feel my Father's benevolent gaze
And He beckons,
"Beloved, come home"

His voice whispers
In the wind
I know somehow
I must get there
And I think,
Can Heaven really be
So close?

But suddenly dark clouds move in
Disturbing my quiet reverie
Destroying my perfect view
The mountain itself
Has disappeared
And I weep
For I can see it no more

The Observatory
Footnote: based on Psalm 1: 6

CONSCIOUSNESS

In this earth-bound existence
Where time flows
And events happen
We cannot fathom
A reality beyond
Our selective and limited view

Truly our perceptions
Are confined by definition
Only to that which we observe

In other dimensions
Heavenly realms exist
Where time and space are not
Only Consciousness
And science admits
There must be an Observer

For something to exist
For everything to exist
For anything to exist

So for Love to be real
For it to be true
An everlasting Intelligence
An omniscient Observer
In stillness, must observe
A Presence animating the Universe

The sacred One
In whom Love defines
The parameters of all true Knowing

<u>I AM</u>
A voice crying in the wilderness
Heard by the One who is
But no one knows the reply
For the sound of it is silence
Yet within the deepest recesses
Of an earnest soul
The Silent One speaks

I AM, He says, I AM

I AM

Footnote: based on John 1: 23, and Exodus 3: 14

WHAT IS ETERNITY FOR?

If you only knew
When he looks at you
Lust is at the door
What would you say?
Would you dress that way?
What is Eternity for?

People are thoughtless
There's so much unrest
Violence, strife, and more
So tell me, friend,
I ask you again,
What is Eternity for?

Religion as hate
Or leave it to fate
Always keeping score
No grace or love
Come down from above,
What is Eternity for?

Evil surrounds me
It's easy to see,
I accept no more!
But what can I say?
When it goes that way,
What is Eternity for?

For sure it's a test
The wages are death
Wretched to the core
What is the plan?
Can you understand?
What is Eternity for?

I wish I could say
That it ends the way
You would not deplore
But believe a lie,
You surely will die,
What is Eternity for?

It is also true
Whatever you do
Goodness can restore
Have faith you must,
In Him shall you trust,
To open Eternity's door!

THEME 13
THE PERFECT GIFT

THE PERFECT GIFT

<u>JUST A KISS</u>

A kiss from you

Is like the cool ocean breeze

On a hot summer day

Like a tasty dessert

After a very good meal

Like a tender caress

That sooths the heart

Like a fragrant flower

That perfumes the air

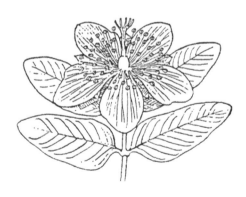

A kiss from you
Is more than a sweet gesture
More than a tender embrace
More than words can express
More than a lover's dream
Your kiss is exuberant joy
Which lights up my every day
Relieves my heavy burden
Heightens my very senses

A kiss from you is
Your most precious gift to me!

GIVE LOVE

Love is pure joy
And pure agony
Choose to embrace them both

Beside Love and Gratitude
There is only Suffering
And the chance to Forgive

All other emotions are unworthy
They are counterfeit
They offer nothing at all

TO AUNT JENNY

It was 47 years ago
When you gave us
Those yellow ceramic bowls

Six in all
A wedding gift

Ever since you departed this life
Do you sometimes gaze down?
Do you sometimes wonder?

If we still like them
If we still use them

Maybe it doesn't matter
Maybe you don't care anymore
About such trivial things

Nevertheless, we do like them
And we do use them

I just thought you would like to know...

LOAVES AND FISHES

He brought loaves and fishes to my door
He gave me them to eat
And so much more
It is certainly Christ whom I adore
He brought loaves and fishes to my door

I have abundant life in His name
Since that day
I'll never be the same
He taught me the reasons why He came
To heal the broken-hearted and the lame

May such bounty as I receive
Overflow to serve
So many in need
May it bring growth and abolish greed
All it takes is to plant a seed

Loaves and Fishes

Footnote: based on Isaiah 61: 1-3 and Matthew 15: 33-38

REJECTED

Why do you not love Me?

I gave you my friendship and a promise of faithfulness

But never did I force my Will

I spread before you the treasures of heaven

And the bounty of earth

But you did not bother to look

I provided food and drink for daily refreshment

And many culinary delights

But you never gave Me thanks

Flowers and birds, I gave for enjoyment

And nature in all her glory

Yet you did not seem to notice

Friends and family

Work and play

Consume all your time

But these too, are gifts
From the One you will not name
From the Friend you do not know

THE PERFECT GIFT
You gave the perfect gift
More radiant than a rainbow
More glorious than a sunset
More fragrant than a flower

This gift, beyond all knowing,
No mind can conceive
No words can express
No heart can fathom

The extension of love is intimacy
The extension of faith is trust
The extension of happiness is joy
The extension of hope is eternal life

THEME 14
JUST FOR FUN

JUST FOR FUN

BE MY SURFBOARD BABY!

Be my surfboard baby
A bright yellow mover
So smooth and so fast
We'll sail past the others
They'll wonder who we are
And marvel at our form

I'll come for the ride baby
The direction's your own
As we weave through the waves
But I'll guide you sometimes
If you should grow weary
Or lose your way

They'll be rough waters baby
I must hold on real tight
Breakers can't pry us apart
The biggest of waves
We'll handle with ease
This skill is taught by love

Be my surfboard baby
I'll wear my bikini
We'll be so finely matched
Adventure awaits us
What fun and what daring
Gliding over the waves!

<u>I LOVE YOU A LATTE</u>

I love you a latte
And I'll tell you why
You're sugar in my coffee
Whipped cream on my pie!

I love you a latte
Because you're just right
Not too sweet or too bitter
Too dark or too light!

Being with you a latte
Is my special treat
Let's go to Maui Roasters
Where true lovers meet!

ON A DIET

Should I eat it?

Do I need it?

Is it good for me?

How I crave it!

Can I save it?

For when I'm diet-free?

Though I diet

Can't I try it?

Specially 'cause it's sweet?

Can I reframe

And not complain

If I skip this treat?

I'm on a diet

I can't deny it

But what's the magic key?

I do my best

I must confess

It's really up to me!

JUST A DOG

In the morning
There she is
Bright eyed and bushy tailed
At 7 am sharp
Ready to start the day

Her front paws hit my pillow
And I see a cute face
Staring back at me
I may even get a lick or two
If I don't get up fast enough

She wants breakfast now!
So she sits at full attention
Almost quivering with excitement
Those big, brown eyes fixated
On my every move

Then at my word
She pops up
Tail wagging furiously
Ready to eat
Ready for adventure!

Her most enduring toy
Is a green stuffed dragon
That she got as a puppy
She also has a blue one
And an aqua one too

But the green one
The most tattered of all
Is the one she nuzzles up to
The one she wrestles with
It's still her favorite toy

When it comes to catching ball
I'm afraid it's hit or miss
Only when a treat's involved
Will she resign herself
To playing this silly, human game

If a stranger comes
She becomes my guard dog
Barking with all the ferociousness she can muster
But she knows when to stop
As soon as the coast is clear

My dog constantly sheds
Rolls in nasty stuff
Chews on dead critters
As if they were chewing gum
And of course, there is doggie poop to pick up

She follows her nose
Wherever it leads
Sometimes to nowhere
Sometimes to deliciousness
Often to disgusting

Alas, she is a dog like any other
Playful and bright
Full of mischief and fun
But she is a dog like no other
My canine masterpiece!

WRITING A POEM

Writing a poem
Is like baking a cake
And putting icing on it
And decorating it
In a particular way
Then eating it
Until it's all gone!

FOOTNOTES

THEME 2 – A Pure Heart

Who is Guilty?

Footnote: based on Luke 23: 34

THEME 5 – The Natural World

It's Spring!

Footnote: written in "Haiku" style

THEME 8 – Suffering

The Crucible

Footnote: based on Sirach 2: 1, 5

THEME 10 – Prayer

Jesus, *please...*

Footnote: based on John 19: 16

THEME 11 – Finding Truth

Where Your Treasure Is

Footnote: based on Matthew 6: 19-21

To My Fellow Christians
Footnote: based on James 2: 10, and 2 Timothy 4: 4

THEME 12 – Eternity
Where Is My Beloved?
Footnote: based on Luke 14: 15

The Observatory
Footnote: based on Psalm 1: 6

I AM
Footnote: based on John 1: 23, and Exodus 3: 14

THEME 13 – The Perfect Gift
Loaves and Fishes
Footnote: based on Isaiah 61: 1-3, and Matthew 15: 33-38

Alda St. James, Author

ABOUT THE AUTHOR

Alda St. James is an artist, poet, counselor, successful master goldsmith and the author of the following books: *"Listen to Love: Reflective Poems for All Seasons"*, *"Wisdom Lessons for Today: Timeless Words of Inspiration & Instructions"*, and *"Birthstone Coloring Book: Birthstone Legends & Other Gem Folklore"*. She holds a Fine Arts degree from Syracuse University and a master's degree in Education and Counseling from the University of Idaho. It has always been her desire to champion the causes of art, beauty, and harmony in everyday life. She does this through many forms of artistic expression, following her intuitive and creative inclinations wherever they lead. The author admits to writing poetry for as long as she can remember. Her Italian name, Alda, means *"richly blessed."* In order to bring more joy and love into the world, Alda and her husband Jim, appreciated the opportunity of becoming foster and adoptive parents. During the years they spent working with abused and neglected children and teens, this effort eventually became their primary mission.

In 2005, with the establishment of the non-profit organization,

"*Keiki Kokua*," Alda and Jim were able to reach many more youth and families. They hosted fun and entertaining activities which helped families thrive despite the rigors and limitations of an overtaxed foster care system. For the St. James, this work was their crowning achievement.

The recent passing of her husband left a huge void in Alda's life. But the loss invited a welcome return to writing, both lyrical poetry and reflective essays on scripture. Being an incurable optimist, the author filled the void with an incredible burst of creative energy, producing an array of poetry that welcomes a promising season of renewal and hope. Today, as an emerging author, Alda has found in writing a source of deep consolation and healing. With this book, the author celebrates her renewed passion as an artist, this time as a crafter of words.

You can learn more about Alda St. James at her website here. aldastjames.com

Made in the USA
Coppell, TX
21 December 2021

69824958R30096